TAMING THE TIGER WITHIN

OTHER BOOKS BY THICH NHAT HANH

Being Peace

Be Still and Know

The Blooming of a Lotus

Breathe! You Are Alive

*Call Me By My True Names:
The Collected Poems of Thich Nhat Hanh*

Cultivating the Mind of Love

For a Future to Be Possible

Fragrant Palm Leaves

Going Home

The Heart of the Buddha's Teaching

The Heart of Understanding

Living Buddha, Living Christ

The Long Road Turns to Joy

Love in Action

The Miracle of Mindfulness

No Death, No Fear

Old Path, White Clouds

The Path of Emancipation

Peace Is Every Step

Present Moment, Wonderful Moment

The Sun My Heart

Taming the Tiger Within

Teachings on Love

Touching Peace

Transformation and Healing

Thich Nhat Hanh

Edited by Pritam Singh

Selections from

No Death, No Fear

Anger

and *Going Home*

TAMING THE TIGER WITHIN

Meditations on Transforming Difficult Emotions

RIVERHEAD BOOKS

New York

RIVERHEAD BOOKS
Published by the Penguin Group
Penguin Group (USA) Inc.
375 Hudson Street, New York, New York 10014, USA
Penguin Group (Canada), 90 Eglinton East, Suite 700, Toronto, Ontario M4P 2Y3, Canada
(a division of Pearson Penguin Canada Inc.)
Penguin Books Ltd., 80 Strand, London WC2R 0RL, England
Penguin Group Ireland, 25 St. Stephen's Green, Dublin 2, Ireland (a division of Penguin Books Ltd.)
Penguin Group (Australia), 250 Camberwell Road, Camberwell, Victoria 3124, Australia
(a division of Pearson Australia Group Pty. Ltd.)
Penguin Books India Pvt. Ltd., 11 Community Centre, Panchsheel Park, New Delhi—110 017, India
Penguin Group (NZ), 67 Apollo Drive, Rosedale, Auckland 0632, New Zealand
(a division of Pearson New Zealand Ltd.)
Penguin Books (South Africa) (Pty.) Ltd., 24 Sturdee Avenue, Rosebank, Johannesburg 2196,
South Africa

Penguin Books Ltd., Registered Offices: 80 Strand, London WC2R 0RL, England

Portions of this book first appeared in *Anger*; *No Death, No Fear*; and *Going Home*.
Copyright © 2004 by Unified Buddhist Church
Cover design by Charles Bjorklund
Cover photo of author by Karen Hagen Liste, courtesy Parallax Press, Berkeley, California
Book design by Amanda Dewey

First Riverhead hardcover edition: October 2004
First Riverhead trade paperback edition: September 2005
Riverhead trade paperback ISBN: 978-1-59448-134-5

The Library of Congress has catalogued the Riverhead hardcover edition as follows:

Nhât Hanh,Thích.
  Taming the tiger within : meditations on transforming difficult emotions /
Thích Nhât Hanh ; edited by Pritam Singh.
     p. cm.
  Selections from the author's Anger; No Death, No Fear; and Going Home.
  ISBN 1-57322-288-7
  1. Buddhism—Psychology. 2. Emotions—Religious aspects—Buddhism.
3. Buddhism—Doctrines. I. Singh, Pritam. II. Title.
BQ4570.P76N53 2004   2004050959
294.3' 44—dc22

PRINTED IN THE UNITED STATES OF AMERICA

29th Printing

Contents

PART I

From Anger to Compassion

I.

Recognition

One of the main causes of our suffering

is the seed of anger inside of us.

Recognize and embrace your anger when it manifests itself. Care for it with tenderness rather than suppressing it.

We are more than our anger,
we are more than our suffering.

Why do you get angry so easily? Is it because your seed of anger is too strong?

If you get angry easily, it may be because the seed of anger in you has been watered frequently over many years, and unfortunately you have allowed it or even encouraged it to be watered.

Many other people, confronted with the same situation, would not get angry like you. They hear the same words, they see the same situation, and yet they are able to stay calm and not get carried away.

Anger has roots in nonanger elements. It has roots in the way we live our daily life. If we take good care of everything in us, without discrimination, we prevent our negative energies from dominating. We reduce the strength of our negative seeds so that they won't overwhelm us.

Before we can make deep changes in our lives,
we have to look into our diet, our way of consuming.
We have to live in such a way that we stop consuming
the things that poison us and intoxicate us. Then,
we will have the strength to allow the best in us
to arise, and we will no longer be victims
of anger, of frustration.

Look at someone who is angry. When you see the tension in her, you become frightened, because the bomb in her may explode any minute.

Whenever anger comes up, take out a mirror and look at yourself. When you are angry, you are not very beautiful, you are not presentable. Hundreds of muscles on your face become very tense. Your face looks like a bomb ready to explode.

When you see your face looking like a bomb ready to explode, you are motivated to do something to change it. You know in your heart what you can do to look more beautiful. You don't need cosmetics. You need only to breathe peacefully, calmly, and to smile mindfully. If you can do that one or two times, you will look much better. Just look in the mirror, breathing in calmly, breathing out smiling, and you will feel relief.

It is very helpful to see yourself in moments when you are angry. It is a bell of mindfulness.

Anger always goes together with confusion,

with ignorance.

Anger is born from ignorance and wrong perceptions. You may be the victim of a wrong perception. You may have misunderstood what you heard and what you saw. You may have a wrong idea of what has been said, what has been done.

Every one of us must practice looking deeply into our perceptions, whether we are a father, mother, child, partner, or friend.

Our body is impermanent, our emotions are impermanent, and our perceptions are impermanent. Our anger, our sadness, our love, our hatred, and our consciousness are also impermanent.

Anger and love are both of an organic nature, and thus they both can change. Hate can always be transformed into love. And unfortunately, many times love is transformed into hate.

Many of us begin a relationship with great love, very intense love. So intense that we believe that, without our partner, we cannot survive. Yet if we do not practice mindfulness, it takes only one or two years for our love to be transformed into hatred. Then, in our partner's presence we have the opposite feeling, we feel terrible. It becomes impossible to live together anymore, so divorce is the only way.

Love has been transformed into hatred; our flower has become garbage.

If you see elements of garbage in you, such as fear, despair, and hatred, don't panic. As a good organic gardener, a good practitioner, you can face this: "I recognize that there is garbage in me. I am going to transform this garbage into nourishing compost that can make love reappear."

Just because anger or hate is present does not
mean that the capacity to love and accept
is not there; love is always in you.

In a time of anger or despair, even if we feel overwhelmed, our love is still there. Our capacity to communicate, to forgive, to be compassionate is still there. You have to believe this. We are more than our anger, we are more than our suffering. We must recognize that we do have within us the capacity to love, to understand, to be compassionate, always.

2.

Care of Anger

The Buddha never advised us to suppress our anger.

He taught us to go back to ourselves and

take good care of it.

It's not healthy to keep your anger inside for long. I always advise my friends, "Do not keep your anger to yourself for more than one day."

As practitioners, we have to be anger specialists.
We have to attend to our anger; we have to
practice until we understand the roots
of our anger and how it works.

Accept your anger because you know,
you understand, that you can take care of it;
you can transform it into positive energy.

Anger is like a howling baby, suffering and crying. Your anger is your baby. The baby needs his mother to embrace him. You are the mother.

Embrace your baby.

Just like our organs, our anger is part of us.
When we are angry, we have to go back to ourselves
and take good care of our anger. We cannot say,
"Go away, anger, I don't want you." When you have
a stomachache, you don't say, "I don't want you
stomach, go away." No, you take care of it.
In the same way, we have to embrace and
take good care of our anger.

When the mother embraces her baby, her energy penetrates him and soothes him. This is exactly what you have to learn to do when anger begins to surface. You have to abandon everything that you are doing, because your most important task is to go back to yourself and take care of your baby, your anger. Nothing is more urgent than taking good care of your baby.

Just embracing your anger, just breathing in
and breathing out, that is good enough.
The baby will feel relief right away.

In the beginning you may not understand the
nature of your anger, or why it has come to be.
But if you know how to embrace it with the
energy of mindfulness, it will begin
to become clear to you.

Mindfulness means to be present, to be aware of what is going on. This energy is very crucial for the practice. The energy of mindfulness is like a big brother or big sister, holding a young one in her arms, taking good care of the suffering child, which is our anger, despair, or jealousy.

Sit and follow your breathing, or practice walking
meditation to generate the energy of mindfulness, and
embrace your anger. After ten or twenty minutes, your
anger will open herself to you, and suddenly you
will see the true nature of your anger.

When we embrace anger and take good care of our anger, we obtain relief. We can look deeply into it and gain many insights. One of the first insights may be that the seed of anger in us has grown too big, and is the main cause of our misery. As we begin to see this reality, we realize that the other person, whom our anger is directed at, is only a secondary cause. The other person is not the real cause of our anger.

When anger manifests in us, we must recognize
and accept that anger is there and that it needs to
be tended to. At this moment we are advised not to
say anything, not to do anything out of anger.
We immediately return to ourselves and invite
the energy of mindfulness to manifest also,
in order to embrace, recognize, and take
good care of our anger.

Practice looking deeply into the nature of your anger. The practice has two phases. The first is embracing and recognizing: "My dear anger, I know you are there, I am taking good care of you." The second phase is to look deeply into the nature of your anger to see how it has come about.

Whether you are driving, walking, cooking, or washing, continue to embrace your anger with mindfulness. By doing so, you have a chance to look deeply into the nature of your anger.

The practices of mindful breathing and mindful walking outdoors are wonderful ways to embrace your anger.

Every mental formation—anger, jealousy, despair, etc.—is sensitive to mindfulness the way all vegetation is sensitive to sunshine. By cultivating the energy of mindfulness, you can heal your body and your consciousness.

People who use venting techniques like hitting a pillow or shouting are actually rehearsing anger. When someone is angry and vents their anger by hitting a pillow, they are learning a dangerous habit. They are training in aggression. Instead, a wise practitioner generates the energy of mindfulness and embraces her anger every time it manifests.

When you cook potatoes, you need to keep the
fire going for at least fifteen or twenty minutes.
You cannot eat raw potatoes. In the same way,
you have to cook your anger on the fire of
mindfulness, and it may take ten minutes,
or twenty minutes, or longer.

Anger is in us in the form of a seed. The seeds of love and compassion are also there. In our consciousness, there are many negative seeds and also many positive seeds. The practice is to avoid watering the negative seeds, and to identify and water the positive seeds every day.

If positive seeds are watered in a person's life,
it is partly because of luck and partly
because of effort.

Sometimes we are overwhelmed by the energy of hate, of anger, of fear. We forget that in us there are other kinds of energy that can manifest also. If we know how to practice, we can bring back the energy of insight, of love, and of hope in order to embrace the energy of fear, of despair, and of anger.

Inside every one of us is a garden, and every practitioner has to go back to their garden and take care of it. Maybe in the past, you left it untended for a long time. You should know exactly what is going on in your own garden, and try to put everything in order. Restore the beauty; restore the harmony in your garden. If it is well tended, many people will enjoy your garden.

With the energy of mindfulness, you can look
into the garbage and say, "I am not afraid.
I am capable of transforming the
garbage back into love."

The energy of mindfulness contains the energy of concentration as well as the energy of insight. Concentration helps you to focus on just one thing. With concentration, the energy of looking becomes more powerful. Because of that, it can make a breakthrough that is insight. Insight always has the power of liberating you. If mindfulness is there, and you know how to keep mindfulness alive, concentration will be there, too. And if you know how to keep concentration alive, insight will come also. So mindfulness recognizes, embraces, and relieves. Mindfulness helps us look deeply in order to gain insight. Insight is the liberating factor. It is what frees us and allows transformation to happen.

This is the practice of taking care of anger.

Every time you feel lost, alienated, or cut off from life, or from the world, every time you feel despair, anger, or instability, practice going home. Mindful breathing is the vehicle that you use to go back to your true home.

3.

Mindfulness of Others

At the moment you become angry, you tend
to believe that your misery has been created by
another person. You blame him or her for all
your suffering. But by looking deeply, you
realize that the seed of anger in you is
the main cause of your suffering.

Even though we are primarily responsible for our own anger, we believe naïvely that if we can say something or do something to punish the other person, we will suffer less.

If your house is on fire, the most urgent thing to do is to go back and try to put out the fire, not to run after the person you believe to be the arsonist. If you run after the person you suspect has burned your house, your house will burn down while you are chasing him or her. That is not the action of a wise person. You must go back and put out the fire. When you are angry, if you continue to interact with or argue with the other person, if you try to punish him or her, you are acting exactly like someone who runs after the arsonist while their home goes up in flames.

Whatever you do or say in a state of anger will only cause more damage in the relationship. Instead, try not to do anything or say anything when you are angry.

In taking good care of yourself, you take good care of your beloved one. Self-love is the foundation for your capacity to love the other person. If you don't take good care of yourself, if you are not happy, if you are not peaceful, you cannot make the other person happy. You cannot help the other person; you cannot love. Your capacity for loving another person depends entirely on your capacity for loving yourself, for taking care of yourself.

When you make another suffer, he or she will try to find relief by making you suffer more.

When you say something unkind, when you
do something in retaliation, your anger increases.
You make the other person suffer, and they try hard
to say or do something back to make you suffer,
and get relief from their suffering. That is
how conflict escalates.

If we really understood and remembered that life
was impermanent, we would do everything we could
to make the other person happy right here and
right now. If we spend twenty-four hours being
angry at our beloved, it is because we are
ignorant of impermanence.

The reason we are foolish enough to make ourselves suffer and make the other person suffer is that we forget that we and the other person are impermanent. Someday, when we die, we will lose all our possessions, our power, our family, everything. Our freedom, peace, and joy in the present moment is the most important thing we have. But without an awakened understanding of impermanence, it is not possible to be happy.

When you try to make each other suffer, the result is an escalation of suffering on both sides. Both of you need compassion and help. Neither of you needs punishment.

When your beloved makes you suffer because she is angry, at first you feel that she deserves punishment. You want to punish her because she has made you suffer. But after ten or fifteen minutes of walking meditation and mindful looking, you realize that what she needs is help and not punishment.

When you get angry with someone, please don't pretend that you are not angry. Don't pretend that you don't suffer. If the other person is dear to you, then you have to confess that you are angry, and that you suffer. Tell him or her in a calm, loving way.

It's very natural that when you suffer, although you know how to practice, you still need the other person to help you in your practice. "Please help me. Darling, I need your help." That is the language of true love.

When you get angry with the other person, you have the tendency to say, "Don't touch me! I don't need you. I can manage very well without you!" But you have made the commitment to take good care of each other.

We are advised to tell the other person that we are angry, that we suffer. "Darling, I suffer, I'm angry, and I want you to know it." Then if you are a good practitioner, you also add, "I'm doing my best to take care of my anger." And you conclude with the third sentence, "Please, do help me," because he or she is still very intimate, very close to you. You still need him or her. Expressing your anger in this way is extremely wise.

You do not have to hide your anger. You have to let the other person know that you are angry and that you suffer. This is very important.

Punishing the other person is self-punishment.

That is true in every circumstance.

If I have a cruel thought or if my words carry hatred in them, then those thoughts and words will be reborn. It will be difficult to catch them and pull them back.

They are like a runaway horse.

In the beginning you told each other, "I cannot live without you. My happiness depends on you." You made declarations like that. But when you are angry, you say the opposite: "I don't need you! Don't come near me! Don't touch me!" You prefer to go into your room and lock the door. You try your best to demonstrate that you don't need the other person. This is a very human, very ordinary tendency. But this is not wisdom.

To say, "Darling, I love you," is good, it is important. It is natural that we share our joy and good feelings with our beloved one. But you also have to let the other person know when you suffer, when you are angry with him or her. You have to express what you feel. You have the right. This is true love. "Darling, I am angry at you. I suffer." Try your best to say it peacefully. There may be some sadness in your voice, that's fine. Just don't say something to punish or to blame. "Darling, I am angry. I suffer, and I need you to know it." This is the language of love, because you have vowed to support each other, as partners, as husband and wife.

If you are capable of writing or saying these three sentences, you are capable of true love. You are using the authentic language of love. "Darling, I suffer, and I want you to know it. Darling, I am doing my best; I'm trying not to blame anyone else, including you. Since we are so close to each other, since we have made a commitment to each other, I feel that I need your support and your help to get out of this state of suffering, of anger." Using the three sentences to communicate with the other person can quickly reassure and relieve him or her. The way you handle your anger will inspire a lot of confidence and respect in the other person, and in yourself.

This is not very difficult to do.

In true love, there is no pride. You cannot pretend
that you don't suffer. You cannot pretend that you are
not angry. This kind of denial is based on pride.
"Angry? Me? Why should I be angry? I'm okay."
But, in fact, you are not okay. You are in hell.
Anger is burning you up, and you must tell
your partner, your son, your daughter.

When you are angry, and you suffer, please go
back and inspect very deeply the content, the nature
of your perceptions. If you are capable of removing
the wrong perception, peace and happiness will
be restored in you, and you will be able to
love the other person again.

Start a peace talk with your beloved one:
"Darling, in the past we have made each other
suffer so much. Both of us were victims of our
anger. We made a hell for each other. Now, I want
to change. I want us to become allies, so that we can
protect each other, practice together, and transform
our anger together. Let us build a better life from
now on, based on the practice of mindfulness.
Darling, I need your help. I need your support. I
need your collaboration. I cannot succeed without
you." You have to say these words to your partner,
your son, your daughter—it's time to do it.
This is awakening. This is love.

Nothing can heal anger except compassion.

Compassion is a beautiful flower born of understanding. When you get angry with someone, practice breathing in and out mindfully. Look deeply into the situation to see the true nature of your own and the other person's suffering, and you will be liberated.

The nectar of compassion is so wonderful. If you are committed to keeping it alive, then you are protected. What the other person says will not touch off the anger and irritation in you, because compassion is the real antidote for anger.

If you allow compassion to spring from your heart,
the fire of anger will die right away.

If it is your partner who is angry, just listen. Listen and do not react. Do your best to practice compassionate listening. Do not listen for the purpose of judging, criticizing, or analyzing. Listen only to help the other person express himself and find some relief from his suffering.

There are many ways to communicate, and the best way is to show that you no longer feel any anger or condemnation. You show that you understand and accept the other person. You communicate this not only by your words but also by your way of being— with your eyes full of compassion and your actions full of tenderness.

When you understand the situation of the other person, when you understand the nature of suffering, anger will vanish, because it is transformed into compassion.

When you begin to see the suffering in the other person, compassion is born, and you no longer consider that person as your enemy. You can love your enemy. The moment you realize that your so called enemy suffers, and you want to help him stop suffering, he ceases to be your enemy.

When we hate someone, and are angry at her, it is
because we do not understand her or the circumstances
she comes from. By practicing deep looking, we realize
that if we grew up like her, in her set of circumstances
and in her environment, we would be just like her.
That kind of understanding removes your anger,
and suddenly that person is no longer your enemy.
Then you can love her. As long as she remains
an enemy, love is impossible.

When you touch the seed of understanding,
mindfulness, and loving-kindness in you, you make
these qualities grow stronger for both your own
happiness and the happiness of other people
and all living beings around you.

Happiness is not an individual matter. If one of you is not happy, it will be impossible for the other person to be happy.

PART II

No Birth, No Death:
From Fear to Love

4.

Fear and Time

As long as fear is still in you,
your happiness cannot be perfect.

We cannot enjoy life if we spend a lot of time worrying about what happened yesterday and what will happen tomorrow. We worry about tomorrow because we are afraid. If we are afraid all the time, we cannot appreciate that we are alive and can be happy now.

When you are carried away with your worries,
fears, cravings, anger, and desire, you run away
from yourself and you lose yourself.

Live your daily life in a way that
you never lose yourself.

We wait for the magical moment—sometime

in the future—when everything

will be as we want it to be.

Life is available only in the present moment.

Please take a pen and a sheet of paper. Go to the foot of a tree or to your writing desk, and make a list of all the things that can make you happy right now: the clouds in the sky, the flowers in the garden, the children playing, the fact that you have met the practice of mindfulness, your beloved ones sitting in the next room, your two eyes in good condition. The list is endless. You have enough already to be happy now. You have enough to no longer be agitated by fear or anger.

A child is always able to live
in the present moment.

The child in us is always alive.

Maybe we have not had enough time
to take care of the child within us.

When we live in the present moment,
it is possible to live in true happiness.

If you can breathe in and out and walk in the spirit of "I have arrived, I am home, in the here, in the now," then you will notice that you are becoming more solid and more free immediately. You have established yourself in the present moment, at your true address. Nothing can push you to run anymore, or make you so afraid. You are free from worrying about the past.

You are not stuck, thinking about what has not happened yet and what you cannot control. You are free from guilt concerning the past, and you are free from your worries about the future.

With mindfulness, you can recognize what is there
in the present moment, including the person you
love. When you can tell your beloved, "Darling, I
know you are there, and I am very happy," it proves
that you are a free person. It proves that you have
mindfulness, you have the capacity to cherish,
to appreciate what is happening in the present
moment. You are still alive, and the person you
love is still there, alive, in front of you.

The circumstances of our lives can help us water the seeds of patience, generosity, compassion, and love. The people around us can help us water these seeds, and so can the practice of mindfulness.

Please remember that your notions of happiness may be very dangerous. The Buddha said happiness can only be possible in the here and now. So go back and examine deeply your notions and ideas of happiness. You may recognize that the conditions of happiness that are already there in your life are enough. Then happiness can be instantly yours.

5.

Finding Refuge,
Knowing Freedom

No fear is the ultimate joy. When you have the insight of no fear, you are free.

The Buddha taught that there is no birth, there is no death; there is no coming, there is no going; there is no same, there is no different; there is no permanent self, there is no annihilation.

Our greatest fear is that when we die

we will become nothing.

People are very afraid of nothingness. When they hear about emptiness, people are also very afraid, but emptiness just means the extinction of ideas. Emptiness is not the opposite of existence. It is not nothingness or annihilation. The idea of existence has to be removed, and so does the idea of nonexistence.

When you practice looking deeply, you see
your true nature of no birth, no death; no being,
no nonbeing; no coming, no going; no same,
no different. When you see this, you are
free from fear. You are free from craving
and free from jealousy.

To really be free of fear, we must look deeply into
the ultimate dimension of no birth, no death.
We need to free ourselves from these ideas that we
are our body, and that we die. This is where
we will discover the place of no fear.

When we understand that we cannot be destroyed,

we are liberated from fear.

If we are able to touch our ground of no birth
and no death, we will have no fear. That is
the base of our true happiness.

To meditate means to be invited on a journey of looking deeply in order to touch our true nature and to recognize that nothing is lost.

We can overcome fear. Nonfear is the greatest gift of meditation. With it we can overcome our grief and our sorrow.

If you have lost someone and if you have cried so very much, please accept the invitation of the Buddha. Look deeply and recognize that the nature of your beloved is the nature of no birth, no death; no coming, no going.

It is only because of our misunderstanding that we think the person we love no longer exists after they "pass away." This is because we are attached to one of the forms, one of the many manifestations of that person. The person we love is still there. He is around us, within us, and smiling at us.

What is the home of a wave? The home of the
wave is all the other waves, and the home of the wave
is water. If the wave is capable of touching himself
and the other waves very deeply, he will realize that
he is made of water. Being aware that he is water, he
transcends all discrimination, sorrows, and fears.

A person who does not have anything to believe in is without energy. When you have the energy of faith in you, your steps become firmer, your look becomes brighter. You are ready to love, to understand, to help, and to work.

There are those who are so discouraged that they no longer have the courage to love. They suffer a great deal just because they made an attempt to love and failed. The wounds within them are so deep that it makes them afraid to try again. We are aware of the presence of these people among us, all around us. We have to bring them the message that love is possible. Our world desperately needs love.

Faith is the outcome of your life. As faith continues to grow, you continue to get the energy, because faith is also an energy like love. If we look deeply into the nature of our love, we will also see our faith. When we have faith in us, we are no longer afraid of anything.

When you have faith, you have a lot of energy.
When you believe in something really good,
true, and beautiful, you are very alive.

If there is a distinction between true love and the kind
of love that can only engender suffering and despair,
the same can be said of faith. There is a kind of faith
that sustains us and continues to give us strength
and joy. Then there is the kind of faith that may
disappear one morning or one evening and
leave us completely lonely and lost.

To meditate means to be invited on a journey of looking deeply in order to touch our true nature and to recognize that nothing is lost.

The amount of happiness that you have
depends on the amount of freedom
that you have in your heart.

The greatest freedoms are freedom from regret,

freedom from fear, freedom from anxiety,

and freedom from sorrow.

Only a free person can be a happy person.

6.

The Love That Springs
from Insight

The practice of mindfulness leads to concentration
and insight. Insight is the fruit of the practice,
which can help us to forgive, to love. In a period of
fifteen minutes, or half an hour, the practice of
mindfulness, concentration, and insight can liberate
you from your anger and turn you into a loving
person. That is the strength of the dharma,
the miracle of the dharma.

A real love letter is made of insight, understanding, and compassion. Otherwise it is not a love letter.

A true love letter can produce a transformation in the other person, and therefore in the world. But before it produces a transformation in the other person, it has to produce a transformation within you. The time you take to write the letter may be your whole life.

Patience is the mark of true love. A father has
to be patient in order to show his love for his son
or daughter. A mother, a son, and a daughter also.
If you want to love, you must learn to be patient.
If you are not patient, you cannot help
the other person.

Understanding is the ground of love.

If a father and son do not understand each other, they will make each other suffer. So understanding is the key that unlocks the door to love.

If understanding is not there, no matter how hard you try, you cannot love. If you say, "I have to try to love him," this is nonsense. You have to understand him, and through understanding, you will be able to love him.

If we live with the understanding of impermanence,

we will cultivate and nurture our love.

Only then will it last.

All the suffering of living beings is our own suffering.

We have to see that we are they and they are us.

When we see their suffering, an arrow of compassion

and love enters our hearts. We can love them, embrace

them, and find a way to help. Only then will we

not be overwhelmed by despair at their

situation. Or our own.

Unless you know how to love your neighbor, you cannot love God. Before placing an offering on the altar of God, you have to reconcile with your neighbor, because reconciling with your neighbor is to reconcile with God. You can only touch God through his creatures; you will not understand what is true love, the love of God, unless you practice the love of humanity.

Love relieves suffering.

Allow yourself to be a torch, and allow the flame

of your torch to be transmitted to other torches.

Practicing like that, you can help peace and

joy grow in the entire world.

This is the practice. When you become mindful, understanding, and loving, you suffer much less, you begin to feel happy, and the people around you begin to profit from your being there.

When you are mindful, you realize that the other person suffers. You see her suffering, and suddenly you don't want her to suffer anymore.

If you touch suffering deeply in yourself and in the other person, understanding will arise. When understanding arises, love and acceptance will also arise, and this will bring the suffering to an end.

When you are motivated by the desire to transcend

suffering, to get out of a difficult situation, and to help

others to do the same, you become a powerful source

of energy that helps you to do what you want to do

to transform yourself and to help other people.

True love is made of understanding—understanding the other person, the object of your love; understanding their suffering, their difficulties, and their true aspiration. Out of understanding there will be kindness, there will be compassion, there will be an offering of joy.

If respect for the other person is no longer there, true love cannot continue for long.

True love is a love without possessiveness. You love and still you are free, and the other person is also free. The kind of love that has no joy is not true love. If both parties cry every day, then that's not true love. There must be joy and freedom and understanding in love.

If mindfulness is cultivated in our daily life,
if concentration and insight are cultivated in our
daily life, we become more open, more tolerant,
and our love grows stronger within us.

Reality cannot be described in terms of being and nonbeing. Being and nonbeing are notions created by you, exactly like the notions of birth and death, coming and going. If your beloved one can no longer be seen, it does not mean that from being she has become nonbeing. If you realize this truth about your beloved, you will suffer much less, and if you realize this truth about yourself, you will transcend your fear of dying,

of nonbeing.